My Fi
about

C7/
C13

Carine Mackenzie

CF4·K

10 9 8 7 6 5 4 3 2 1
© Copyright 2013 Carine Mackenzie
ISBN: 978-1-78191-123-5
Published by
Christian Focus Publications,
Geanies House, Fearn,
Ross-shire, IV20 1TW, U.K.

Unless stated, the Scripture quotations in this book are
based on the English Standard Version of the Scriptures.

www.christianfocus.com
email:info@christianfocus.com

Cover design by Alister MacInnes and
Daniel van Straaten
All illustrations by Diane Mathes

Printed and bound by Bell and Bain, Glasgow

Contents

What is the Word of God like?

Introduction

God has given us a wonderful gift, the Bible. This is an amazing book, written by about forty different people, each one inspired by God, the Holy Spirit. So it is one complete book – God is the author.

The Bible is also known as the Scripture, which means writings. God's Word has been written down and preserved through the centuries. Some was written in Hebrew and some in Greek, but it has been translated into many languages and we have it now in our own language.

Old Testament

The Bible is divided into two sections, called the Old Testament and the New Testament. The Old Testament has thirty-nine books originally written in the Hebrew language.

Jesus knew these Scriptures very well and quoted from them.

He fulfilled the prophecy about himself in his life and death and resurrection.

The Old Testament points to the Lord Jesus – the Son of God who came to earth as a human with the purpose of saving his people from their sins.

New Testament

The New Testament has twenty-seven books originally written in Greek.

The Gospels tell about Jesus' life and ministry.

Acts records the beginning of the Christian church.

The Epistles are the teaching of the apostles to the early church.

Revelation is a prophetic book, revealing future events.

Each book is now divided into chapters. Each chapter is divided into verses. This makes it easier for us to find a particular sentence in the book.

What is the Word of God?

1. The Word of God is true

Your word is truth. John 17:17

And now, O Lord God, you are God, and your words are true. 2 Samuel 7:28

Every word of God proves true. Proverbs 30:5

God is a God of truth. He does not lie, or exaggerate or try to deceive anyone.

His Word, the Bible, is completely true. In court, a witness promises to tell the truth, the whole truth and nothing but the truth. God is the most faithful witness.

The Lord Jesus told us that one of his names is 'The Truth' (John 14:6). We can trust him completely.

2. The Word of God lasts forever

Heaven and earth will pass away, but my words will not pass away.
Mark 13:31

The grass withers, the flower fades, but the word of our God will stand forever.
Isaiah 40:8

The clothes you have today will one day wear out. Your toys will break and be thrown away. The flowers in the garden wither and die. God tells us that even the world we live in, will be burned up and come to an end.

But God's Word will never be destroyed. It will last forever.

3. The Word of God is pure

The words of the Lord are pure words, like silver refined in a furnace.
Psalm 12:6

After silver is mined from the ground, it is melted and heated to a very high temperature. The impurities rise to the surface and the silversmith scoops them off.

Eventually the silver is pure and shining.

God's Word is like that pure silver. No impurities spoil the perfection.

We are sinners; our lives are not pure.

Jesus shed his blood on the cross and the blood of Jesus Christ, God's Son, cleanses us from all sin.

4. The Word of God is living and active

The word of God is living and active, sharper than any two-edged sword ... discerning the thoughts and intentions of the heart. Hebrews 4:12

God's Word is not merely a collection of stories and interesting facts. God's Word works. It reaches into a person's mind and heart and convinces of sin. It persuades us that the only way to be truly happy is to trust in the Lord Jesus, who died on the cross to forgive our sins.

It prods our conscience to correct us when we do wrong. It helps us to praise and thank God for his grace and love and mercy.

5. The Word of God is perfect

The law of the Lord is perfect, reviving the soul.
Psalm 19:7

We are all born as sinners, natural enemies of God. To be right with God, our lives have to be turned around from loving sin to trusting in

the Lord Jesus Christ. This is called conversion.

God's Holy Spirit works in the heart and soul. God's Word is the ideal, perfect means to bring about this change.

6. The Word of God is inspired

All Scripture is breathed out by God and profitable for teaching, for reproof, for correction, and for training in righteousness.
2 Timothy 3:16

The Bible writers, like Matthew, Paul and Isaiah wrote their books not because they thought it would be a good idea.

They were moved by the Holy Spirit to speak from God. God inspired the Bible writers. He breathed out his thoughts and words into their minds and they wrote it down. This makes the Bible a unique book.

7. The Word of God has no errors

Every word of God proves true; he is a shield to those who take refuge in him.
Proverbs 30:5

The Bible is completely true and without error in any part. Someone who copied or translated the manuscript could make a mistake, but the original, as God first gave

it, is always correct. To disbelieve the Bible is to disbelieve God. God cannot lie. His Word, the Bible, does not lie either.

Two big words describe this –

The Bible is **infallible** – always right and true.
The Bible is **inerrant** – never makes a mistake.

We can completely trust God and his Word.

8. The Word of God is a name given to the Lord Jesus

The name by which he is called is The Word of God.
Revelation 19:13

In the beginning was the Word, and the Word was with God, and the Word was God.
John 1:1

The Word of God is one of the names given to God the Son, who came to this world to be the Saviour of sinners. He was born in Bethlehem, and given the name Jesus. He lived as a man in our world. But he never ceased to be God the Son, who has existed from all eternity. This is an amazing truth which should make us want to worship him.

What does the Word of God do?

9. The Word of God created everything

By faith we understand that the universe was created by the word of God.
Hebrews 11:3

God created the whole world by his powerful Word. God said, 'Let there be light,' and there was light. God said, 'Let the waters under the heavens be gathered into one place, and let the dry land appear.' And it was so.

God said, 'Let the earth sprout vegetation' and it was so. God said, 'Let there be lights in the heavens' and it was so. With a word, God created birds, sea creatures and animals.

10. The Word of God teaches us what to believe about God

You search the Scriptures because you think that in them you have eternal life; and it is they that bear witness about me.
John 5:39

The Bible teaches us about God. It tells us what he is – holy, powerful, good, just, wise, loving. The Bible

teaches us what God has done for us – giving us life, breath, food, shelter, family – and a Saviour, the Lord Jesus, to deal with our sin and grant us forgiveness.

The Old Testament stories and prophecies point to the coming Saviour; the Gospels tell about his life and death; the Epistles tell of how Jesus' life and death make all the difference to us.

11. The Word of God makes us wise for salvation

And how from childhood you have been acquainted with the sacred writings, which are able to make you wise for salvation through faith in Christ Jesus.
2 Timothy 3:15

The Lord Jesus came to this world to be the Saviour of sinners. God tells us about his Son, the Saviour, in his Word. We learn about his plan of salvation in the Bible. It speaks God's message to our heart – convincing us of our sin and assuring us of God's grace and mercy. This makes us wise for salvation.

12. The Word of God teaches us what we ought to do

Let us hear the conclusion of the whole matter: Fear God, and keep his commandments: for this is the whole duty of man.
Ecclesiastes 12:13 (KJV)

The great, holy God, our Creator, requires us to be obedient to him and his law. This is given to us in detail in the Bible. We must honour and respect God and live in a way that is pleasing to him.

Often we fall into sin and wish to please ourselves. God's Word challenges us and calls us back to God. Jesus kept the law perfectly and we must trust in him.

13. The Word of God is a purifier

How can a young man keep his way pure? By guarding it according to your word.
Psalm 119:9

If we ignore God's Word, we will soon be taken over by sin. We will think bad thoughts; we will say wrong words – lies and boasting and unkindness; we will do sinful actions. Only the Lord through his word can keep a person, young or old, from falling into the sin that stains our life.

14. The Word of God gives joy to the heart

Your words became to me a joy and the delight of my heart.
Jeremiah 15:16

If we love the Lord, we love to read or listen to his Word. It brings a lasting joy and satisfaction as it tells us about what Jesus Christ has done for us and continues to do for us. This joy makes us want to praise God and thank him for his love and goodness to us.

15. The Word of God is hidden in the heart

I have stored up your word in my heart, that I might not sin against you.
Psalm 119:11

It is a good thing to memorise verses from the Bible. When we are tempted to sin, God's word will

strengthen us and keep us from telling a lie or stealing or any of the sins that can bother us.

If we know some verses off by heart we can think about them as we lie in bed in the dark.

God the Holy Spirit brings to our minds the word that we have learned.

What is the Word of God like?

16. The Word of God is like a seed

Jesus said, 'The seed is the word of God.'
Luke 8:11

Jesus told a story comparing the Word of God to seeds. When the farmer sowed the seed it fell on different types of ground. Some withered and died, but some multiplied and grew and produced more grain. When you hear the Word of God, does it flourish and produce in your heart the fruit of the Spirit like love, joy, and peace?

If we ignore the Word of God or think that other things are more important, then we do not produce good fruit in our lives.

17. The Word of God is like a sword

Take the helmet of salvation, and the sword of the Spirit, which is the word of God.
Ephesians 6:17

A soldier has to be armed. Long ago he would use a sword to fight the enemy. The Christian has an enemy too – the devil. We must always be ready to use our sword, the Word of God, to fight against the devil. Jesus used the Word of God to defeat the devil who was tempting him to sin. Three times he said, 'It is written ...' and quoted a verse from the book of Deuteronomy. (See Luke chapter 4:1-13).

18. The Word of God is like a fire

'Is not my word like fire?' declares the Lord.
Jeremiah 23:29

A fire can sweep through a forest or a building, destroying everything in its path. God's Word is as powerful as a fire. It pronounces judgement on people who hate God or ignore God and his law. God's judgement is perfect and just and certain for those who refuse God and his Word. Jesus Christ has taken the punishment for the sin of those who trust in him.

19. The Word of God is like food

I have not departed from the commandment of his lips; I have treasured the words of his mouth more than my portion of food.
Job 23:12

Job, who lived many years ago, had lots of problems. His family were killed, his possessions destroyed; his body covered with horrible

boils. His wife was no help, nor were his friends. But Job could say that he loved God's words more than his necessary food.

Without food we could not live. The Bible, God's Word, gives nourishment and life to our souls.

Food in the fridge does not nourish our body. We have to eat it to get any benefit.

The Bible sitting on the shelf does us no good. We have to read it or listen to it to see an effect in our daily lives.

20. The Word of God is like a hammer

Is not my word ... like a hammer that breaks the rock in pieces?
Jeremiah 23:29

The pounding of a sledge hammer can break strong rock in pieces. The truth of God's Word is strong and can break the hardest heart

and change the sinner. When God converts the sinner, he gives him a new heart to love and trust him.

God's Word cannot be broken – even when evil people misuse it or tell lies about it – God's Word, like a hammer, will destroy that falsehood.

21. The Word of God is like a lamp

Your word is a lamp to my feet and a light to my path.
Psalm 119:105

If you go out walking on a dark night, it is wise to take a torch with you. The bright light dispels the darkness and helps you on your way. In the dark we are more likely to stumble and fall.

God's Word is like a lamp, guiding us on the right way and keeping us from falling into temptation and sin. The words of the Bible dispel the darkness of sin and guide us on our journey through life.

22. The Word of God is like milk

Like newborn infants, long for the pure spiritual milk, that by it you may grow up into salvation.
1 Peter 2:2

When a baby cries, it is often because he is hungry and is longing

for some milk. When he gets it, he is happy. It is the regular feeding with milk that makes him grow.

Regularly reading or hearing God's Word helps us to grow in grace and in the knowledge of God. If we are starved of God's Word, our spiritual life will suffer and make us unhappy. But God's Word will satisfy our souls and do us good.

23. The Word of God is like solid food

Everyone who lives on milk is unskilled in the word of righteousness, since he is a child. But solid food is for the mature.
Hebrews 5:13-14

Babies drink milk, but as we grow up, we move on to solid food, like meat and vegetables.

When we are young, we learn about God's Word – starting with the simple things.

As we grow older, we will want to learn more and more.

Even the oldest, cleverest person will always find something to learn in God's Word.

24. The Word of God is more precious than gold

(The words of the Lord are) more to be desired than gold, even much fine gold.
Psalm 19:10

Gold is a precious and beautiful metal which is made into coins, jewellery and other lovely things. A rich man will own lots of precious gold items.

The Word of God is even more valuable. God has given us this amazing gift and we should value it more than any gold object we possess.

25. The Word of God is sweeter than honey

(The words of God are) sweeter also than honey and drippings of the honeycomb.
Psalm 19:10

Honey, made by the bees, is delicious and so sweet. It is nourishing and sustaining and very pleasant to taste.

God's Word is so good to read and to think about. It gives us strength for our daily life, comfort in sadness and satisfies all our needs.

From the Author

God has graciously given us his Word, which has been preserved by him through the ages and translated into a language that we can understand. What a precious gift!

In it God tells us all that we need to believe about him. It tells us the gospel of the Lord Jesus Christ who is the only way of salvation from sin, leading to eternal life.

God's Word teaches us what kind of behaviour God asks of us, in order to serve and glorify him.

My prayer is that this little book will cause you to see just how valuable the Bible is and help you to praise and thank God for his kindness and love.

Carine Mackenzie

OTHER BOOKS IN THE SERIES

My 1st Book of Bible Prayers, Philip Ross
ISBN: 978-1-85792-944-7

My 1st Book of Bible Promises,
Carine Mackenzie
ISBN: 978-1-84550-039-9

My 1st Book of Christian Values,
Carine Mackenzie
ISBN: 978-1-84550-262-1

My 1st Book of Memory Verses,
Carine Mackenzie
ISBN: 978-1-85792-783-2

My 1st Book about the Church,
Carine Mackenzie
ISBN: 978-1-84550-570-7

My 1st Book of Questions and Answers,
Carine Mackenzie
ISBN: 978-1-85792-570-8

My 1st Book about Jesus, Carine Mackenzie
ISBN: 978-1-84550-463-2

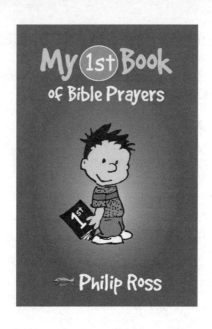

My 1st Book of Bible Prayers, Philip Ross
ISBN: 978-1-85792-944-7

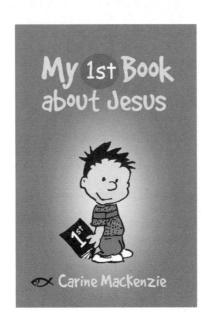

My 1st Book about Jesus, Carine Mackenzie
ISBN: 978-1-84550-463-2

CHRISTIAN FOCUS PUBLICATIONS

Christian   Christian   CF4K   Mentor
Focus   Heritage

Christian Focus Publications publishes books for adults and children under its four main imprints: Christian Focus, CF4K, Mentor and Christian Heritage. Our books reflect our conviction that God's Word is reliable and Jesus is the way to know him, and live for ever with him.

Our children's publication list includes a Sunday School curriculum that covers pre-school to early teens, and puzzle and activity books. We also publish personal and family devotional titles, biographies and inspirational stories that children will love.

If you are looking for quality Bible teaching for children then we have an excellent range of Bible stories and age-specific theological books.

From pre-school board books to teenage apologetics, we have it covered!

Find us at our web page:
www.christianfocus.com

CF4•K
Because you're never
too young to know Jesus